6 Steps to Retirement

A Logical and Sequential Approach to Planning Your Retirement

By Michael Graff

Printed in the United States of America
ISBN: 9781796519457

Edited by Lisa Neuberger
Cover Design & Interior Formatting by Lisa Neuberger
lneuberger.writer@gmail.com

To my mother, Marylyn Graff

She was a loving and thoughtful mom who was always there for her family and friends. She lived her life to the fullest and is loved, missed, and always remembered…

MICHAEL GRAFF

 Mike is a veteran of several decades of helping people in various aspects of personal and business financial services, including real estate finance, insurance, investments, and income taxes. He is an independent financial services professional and owner of ProIncome, a Massachusetts-based planning firm with a focus on providing professional retirement income planning and investment management. In addition to his client services work, Mike speaks to various groups on Social Security, retirement income tax planning, estate planning, long term care, and retirement income distribution strategies. He is an Investment Advisor Representative with a Series 65 Securities License and a Chartered Tax Advisor®

Table of Contents

PREFACE

Writing a book was never something I seriously considered doing, but about a year ago it occurred to me I had something to say that went beyond my everyday responsibilities as a retirement planning professional. People seemed receptive to my advice, planning tools, and the process I offered, responding with such positive feedback that I realized I was onto something unique, measurable, and repeatable. I began to assemble and organize my concepts, writing them all down in such a way that it eventually took the form of this book.

6 Steps to Retirement comes from my thirty-five years (and counting) working with and observing people and their money. From real estate finance to insurance and investments, it became clear to me that people are generally ambiguous, apprehensive, and otherwise lacking confidence in matters of money.

This is particularly true when it comes to preparing financially for retirement. The purpose of this book is to help people be more proactive with their retirement planning by offering an organized and sequential process designed to aid in transitioning to and succeeding in retirement.

In today's complex and ever-changing economic environment, it isn't difficult to understand the financial exasperation expressed by so many people. From a lack of financial education during our formative years, to the avalanche of financial information from countless media sources, it's no wonder people are mostly confused about the steps to take with their money. The government is certainly no help, nor is the financial services industry, including banking, insurance, and investment companies, that tend to focus more on profits than the people they serve as clients.

While I cannot suggest solutions for fixing financial education, nor offer options to change the way the media or financial services industry conduct themselves, what I can offer with this book is a way for you, as a user of money and as a consumer of financial services, to organize, better understand, and manage your financial and income resources for long term financial success.

6 Steps to Retirement is written for those approaching and living in retirement. It outlines a financial management and retirement planning approach I tag "6 Steps Retirement." It is a retirement planning process intended to be organized in its approach and sequential in its execution.

Like any activity we attempt to do well in life, proper money management and retirement planning requires organization to better understand and evaluate financial resources, and the tasks needed to bring about a high degree of financial efficiency must be completed in a proper sequence. I outline six distinct and essential categories of information that should be addressed within the scope of a retirement plan. I then label them as "steps" in order to emphasize the need for addressing each in proper sequence.

"6 Steps Retirement" is a method to help you develop and maintain an effective and efficient retirement plan but with the understanding that any plan you make today is based on the current conditions and circumstances of your life and the economy. As your life and economy evolve over time, re-evaluations and adjustments to existing plans will need to be made.

I hope this book helps you quiet the financial noise, better understand your financial circumstances and options, and move forward confidently with your retirement planning, which will ultimately help you achieve your desired retirement lifestyle.

INTRODUCTION

When it comes to your retirement—or anyone's retirement for that matter—there is no shortage of information and advice. It seems that every financial services firm, discount broker, wealth manager, life insurer, bank, and mutual fund company is pitching some kind of financial product or service having to do with retirement. They all want to help you plan, save, and invest for your golden years. In fact, there are almost as many television ads for these retirement services providers as there are for Flo from Progressive and the Geico Gecko.

In any case, retirement is big business. Why? Because there's a lot of money to be made in fees, premiums, and commissions, and the more of your retirement nest-egg you hand over to any one of these helpful, neighborhood retirement services companies, the more each of them will make.

They're after your money...

Whatever you have saved for your retirement, these retirement service companies want it—all of it. They will entice you with their particular brand of information and advice, and they will be relentless in their pursuit. In the end, they will probably get it, most of it anyway. Oh hell, they really already have it. It started more than thirty years ago with the advent of the 401k and the Individual Retirement Account (IRA). Back in the early 1980s, these types of retirement savings vehicles, and others that have followed, started vacuuming up your retirement money, and as it stands today, the vast majority of most everyone's retirement savings is parked in one of these tax qualified/tax deferred accounts. We are talking trillions and trillions of dollars, and this kind of money will generate a lot of earnings for these retirement money-focused companies.

And the beat goes on…

In addition to the avalanche of self-promotion from these retirement product providers, financial information of all kinds is coming at us from numerous outlets (TV, radio, social media, books, newspapers, and magazines) and being offered by a myriad of financial experts and pundits espousing their opinions and brands of advice. Additionally, there are a multitude of stock market reports and predictions, domestic and international economic news items, and various opinions on money and retirement promulgated by family, friends, co-workers, and even the person we sat next to on the plane or train recently.

Retirement insecurity…

Despite this abundance of retirement assistance, information, and advice, the number of us feeling good about retiring is somewhat low. According to the 2017 Retirement Confidence Survey by the Employee Benefit Research Institute, only 18% of American workers feel very confident about having enough money for retirement. This is down from 21% the previous year. Another 42% report having a lesser degree of retirement confidence, while the remaining 40% are not confident at all. Overall, retirement confidence is declining.

It seems that all this retirement assistance, information, and advice we are privy to isn't really helping. In my role, admittedly, as one of these retirement services professionals, I see and hear about this all the time—people expressing confusion and concern about retirement. While this sentiment represents an opportunity for us retirement planning professionals, the bottom line is many people know they are not financially prepared to retire, and it is weighing on them heavily and taking an emotional toll. It's also unfortunate that even those who do have a measurable level of retirement confidence are still concerned they are not properly managing their retirement assets and that this could ultimately jeopardize their retirement plans and security.

Drinking from a firehose...

In my role as a retirement services professional, I, too, dole out a fair amount of retirement information and advice to my clients. I believe that my advice is of value to them, but it does mean I am adding to the same avalanche of retirement information I call into question. In fact, it is not farfetched to believe the reason for most everyone's lack of retirement confidence is their inability to take in all the information being rained down on them and then make sense of it all.

In my case, and in my defense, I believe the information I provide to my clients is educational and helpful as a way for them to more clearly see and understand their financial options for retirement. Regardless, it is a tremendous challenge these days with the veritable smorgasbord of retirement information being served up for anyone to truly figure things out and feel completely confident about their retirement.

Buyer beware...

As I've stated, an overabundance of financial marketing and information overwhelms many of us, and recognizing my role in all this as a contributor, I have worked to provide information I feel is educational and helpful. In contrast, much of what is being thrust upon us by the financial and insurance industries and related experts and pundits is not educational or helpful, but instead is oriented toward specific products they want you to purchase and/or invest in. In fact, this is where the wheels fall off the bus for many people.

They are confronted with investment and insurance products to consider and acquire before they ever do any kind of substantive financial or retirement planning. It seems to be a mad race by financial and insurance companies to vacuum up our retirement money by presenting products of numerous designs and gimmicks with little, if any, emphasis on helping to develop an actual plan that would make good use of those products. Now, that may be fine for them because they will earn profits from all the fees, premiums, and commissions derived from selling these products, but it certainly has been leaving many of us confused and insecure about retiring. In other words, people are being presented with all the parts needed to build a secure retirement, but are left without instructions on how to assemble these parts into a functioning and secure retirement design.

Retirement blueprint...

As an example, let's say you want to build a house. You could start by going to the lumber yard and buying all the wood, nails, concrete, shingles, insulation, doors and windows, and everything else needed to build your house, but would you know how much of each to buy, or how to put all this together to build the house you want? Alternately, you could start by hiring an architect to develop a set of plans for the house you want. Your architect would start by asking you questions to better understand what kind of home you want and how to design it to suit your lifestyle, then develop a set of blueprints containing all the information you need to purchase the right materials in the right quantities for your new home. Your architect would then help you acquire everything you need and supervise the construction of your new home.

Connecting the parts...

Continuing the analogy, without a clear blueprint, your new home will not likely be what you want or need. In fact, as hard as you might try to put it all together, it would likely fail to provide an adequate roof over your head to protect you from the harsh elements. It's the same with retirement. Without a carefully conceived retirement plan, there's a good chance you will acquire, and may already have acquired, the wrong or less effective financial products for your retirement portfolio and plan.

During initial meetings with clients, I have heard many complain about having acquired an investment or insurance product they either feel was the wrong thing to buy, couldn't recall why they bought it, or the product did not do what they thought it would. These same people almost always admitted they did not have any kind of retirement plan in place to guide them regarding which products they should own and how to go about acquiring them. Most often they simply reacted to a product solicitation from a financial or insurance salesperson and agreed to buy it without a clear idea of how it would help them in retirement.

The result of all this? Many people make ineffective or poor financial decisions that can be—and often are—very costly to the point that they will not achieve financial security in retirement. Or worse, they end up having to make unfortunate sacrifices to their retirement lifestyle. This is very troubling.

For the most part, people understand they should plan for their retirement, but they are not being offered the opportunity from their respective financial/ insurance salespeople to develop a real retirement plan—a plan that clearly shows, step by step, how to build a financially secure retirement.

Who is the architect of your retirement?

Early in my career I was a little guilty of being one of these money-products pushers. Not because I made a conscious decision to be a salesperson of this variety, but simply because I didn't know any better. In my industry, the day we are hired by the typical investment or insurance company, we are taught to learn all about the products and told to go out and make sales, usually to your circle of family, friends, and acquaintances.

My objective here is not to lambast the financial and insurance industries; after all, they must earn money and make a profit, too. The point I want to make is that people need to have a retirement plan in place before considering and acquiring the products and services that serve to support a good retirement plan. Otherwise, they will either acquire the wrong products and/or mismanage the products they already own.

The investment, financial services, and insurance industries are comprised of profit seeking enterprises that make their money by selling products. The majority of these companies do not make money by *planning*; they make money by *selling*. I'm not suggesting this is the case 100% of the time, but I can attest, from firsthand experience, that financial and insurance salespeople are trained to close product sales with little, if any, training on how to do planning. Teaching "closing" techniques is as much a part of training in the financial and insurance industries as it is in many other sales-driven-products industries. Again, this is not a bad thing as much as it is a "buyer beware" thing. What is important for people to understand is that they should not purchase financial, investment, or insurance products unless it is part of an overall plan or strategy that has been arrived at by way of a process that carefully assesses needs and lifestyle objectives.

The shortest distance between two points…

At this point I have stated my case for why people are generally confused and concerned about retirement. I have also called into question the financial and insurance industries for being overly product-oriented. On both points, I contend the resolution is for people to embark on a planning process that will put them in a position to knowledgeably and confidently acquire the right financial and insurance products and that this ultimately will alleviate their financial and retirement anxiety.

I refer to this as being financially "proactive" as opposed to being "reactive."

Taking charge…

By definition, proactive people approach things with a purpose and a plan. Reactive people deal with things as they come up. To be proactive regarding your retirement planning requires, first and foremost, having a clear vision of how you want to live your retirement. The reactive person has no retirement vision—just an idea that someday they would like to retire.

Proactive People

- know their net worth, what it is comprised of, and how it is trending in terms of growth.
- know how well their investments are performing, how much risk is present in their investment allocations, what they are paying in fees and why, what their taxes are, etc.
- know how much money is coming in and going out, understand cash flow, and have some type of budget and spending plan that prioritizes saving money, the proper use of credit, and living within their means.
- understand that things can go wrong and that they can suffer unexpected expenses or circumstances that are outside their cash-flow means. They are prepared financially to address emergencies and have the right kinds of insurance in place to mitigate all known risks.
- have an estate plan in place that is updated regularly to adjust to changing life circumstances. This means having a Will, Advanced Healthcare Directive, Power of Attorney, a Trust (if needed), etc. They have communicated with their families, friends, and others who need to know how they want things to occur and how their remaining assets are to be managed and/or distributed in the event they become incapacitated or die unexpectedly.

Reactive People

- are unclear about the details of their money and investments, and have only a vague sense of what it's all worth.
- are unsure about how their investments are performing, how much risk is present in their investment allocations, what they are paying in fees and why, what their taxes are, etc.
- hope they have some money left over from their paycheck at the end of the month, and if so, probably spend it on the next thing they want, without giving much thought to saving any of it.
- don't have an emergency fund, and if there is a financial crisis, large or small, they probably have to resort to borrowing money or other drastic means to deal with it. They are also much more prone to running out of money during retirement.
- have either no estate plan or an outdated or incomplete plan that leaves them and their family unprepared to deal with incapacity or end-of-life issues, often resulting in disagreements among family and friends that can and often times do lead to costly legal entanglements.

Who are you?

So…are you "proactive" or "reactive"? If you're like most people, you are both to one degree or the other. Obviously, we should all be as proactive as possible and are hopefully working toward this, but the question is what kinds of things should you be doing to be more proactive to achieve a secure retirement and in what order or sequence? Again, there are many financial and insurance professionals who are only too happy to tell you what to do and what investment and insurance products to acquire, but being successful at achieving a financially secure retirement by relying on the counsel of some financial or insurance company professional presupposes they will offer you a retirement plan first. Frankly and unfortunately, this is not likely to happen. Again, financial, investment, insurance professionals typically get paid for selling products, not for planning. What you need to do is understand the planning process for yourself, so you will be ready and able to act proactively to acquire and properly manage the investment and insurance products you need to make your retirement plan function properly.

A long journey is made up of small steps...

Unfortunately, there is no escaping the fact that retirement preparedness does encompass a lot of things. Much must be considered to make sure you have sufficient financial resources to establish and maintain your desired retirement lifestyle.

Recognizing this, I have put together what I believe is a way to quiet the noise, sift through the data, evaluate the options, recognize the opportunities, and ultimately develop a sound retirement plan and strategy that will offer a predictable, sufficient, and sustainable retirement income. You will raise your level of retirement confidence to the highest possible level and will be able to establish a plan that will have you living your desired retirement lifestyle with the confidence that your money will last as long as you do.

It starts with following 6 essential steps set up to be straight-forward, organized, sequential, and doable. Let us proceed.

The 6 Steps

These are the six sequential and necessary steps to developing an effective and efficient retirement plan that will help you to live your desired retirement lifestyle.

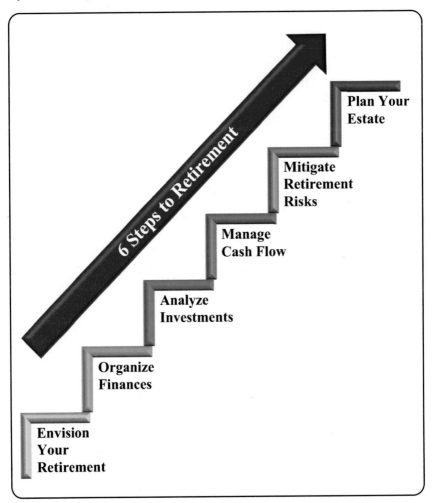

Let's review each of these steps in depth to provide the framework for how to adapt them to your retirement circumstances and objectives.

Step 1

Envision Your Retirement

It's not all about the money...

This step is what the vast majority of retirement planning professionals completely miss. They believe retirement is all about the money, and they jump right in talking to you about investment and insurance products. Of course, it's important to address these items, but not before discussing what you want and need those products for. In other words, you've been saving all this money for a long time for your retirement, but what do you want and need to spend it on? What do you want to do, experience, and accomplish during your retirement years? It really makes no sense to be doing financial planning until you have a clear idea of how you want to spend your money.

Dreams can come true...

You must begin the planning process by thinking about what you want for your retirement. Forget about the money for the moment, and let your mind wander. Really think about all the things you've dreamed about doing and having during your life, but were too busy with work and family to have the time and/or money to make happen.

This is an area of planning where a financial advisor like me may not be able to offer that much help. My role here is more of a facilitator, making general suggestions and encouraging my clients to get in touch with their *inner retired self*—to explore their hopes and dreams. I urge them to get creative about deciding what things and experiences they most want to have and do during their golden years.

The Bucket List...

Think about where you want to live and spend your time. Do you want to be with family? Do some traveling? Perhaps begin a second career doing work that would be more meaningful? Do you want to golf, fish, hike, bike, skydive, and do other activities or hobbies? Do you want to participate in volunteer work? Catch up on reading? Take classes? Explore your artistic side? Do you want to own an RV, boat, or motorcycle?

I'm not suggesting that you will be able to do or afford everything on your bucket list, but write everything down and believe that with the right kind of planning, you can, and will, check off more bucket list items than you thought possible!

Step 2

Organize Finances

For every minute spent organizing, an hour is earned.
–Benjamin Franklin

This is perhaps the most important step. It is the one area where almost everyone struggles and can use some help. I find that in almost every case, when a person or couple has their financial house in order, they always feel better and more empowered to consider financial options and opportunities and ultimately, to make good decisions that result in positive outcomes and financial gains.

Financial organization is the process of pulling together everything you have, so you know what you have, where it all is, and how much it's all worth. It's like a puzzle that comes in a box with a picture on the front, showing what all the pieces will look like when put together. When you first open the box and dump the pieces out onto a table, it's a jumble and looks like nothing. You start by finding the four corner pieces. Then you find and assemble the edge pieces. Finally, you put together all the middle pieces until the puzzle is completed and looks like the picture on the box.

Think of the picture on the box as your Retirement Vision. All your financial resources are the pieces that will make it possible to see the picture and achieve your vision. The task at hand is to make sure you have all the pieces you need to form the picture then put them together.

Taking an inventory...

Begin by completing an inventory of all your financial holdings, income resources, assets, and debts and liabilities. This includes holdings owned in various asset classes (bank holdings, stocks, bonds, real estate, life insurance and annuities, precious metals and commodities, collectibles, etc), income resources such as Social Security and pensions, and both short and long-term liabilities. The main objective is to clearly see and understand what you have, where it is, and what it all adds up to.

This may seem somewhat basic, even unnecessary, but when I supervise this activity for clients, it is almost always an eye-opening experience. Most people have only a general or vague idea of what their holdings comprise. Upon completion of this step, many people are pleasantly surprised at what they actually have and how much it's worth, and in some instances, people uncover assets they had forgotten about or misplaced.

As soon as all the assets are pulled together and inventoried, you need to calculate your Net Worth. This is the sum total of assets minus liabilities. Net Worth is a very important number. It represents the entirety of all financial decisions you have made over the years, both good and not so good. More importantly, it is the primary number I use on an ongoing basis to track how effectively my clients are managing their financial resources, or how effectively their resources are being managed for them, if they are using a third party financial/investments manager. In either case, use this initial net worth as a benchmark to refer back to periodically to assess your financial condition and progress.

Here's what is important to understand about Net Worth: It will do one of three things over time.

 ## Net Worth Will INCREASE

Over time, money will flow onto your balance sheet from various sources, including paychecks, interest, dividends, appreciation of investments, etc. By contrast, you will have money flowing out to cover the costs necessary to pay bills and otherwise maintain your standard of living and enjoy life.

Assuming the flow of money coming in exceeds the flow of money going out on a consistent basis, and your holdings appreciate in value, your Net Worth will rise steadily over time.

This Net Worth trend is obviously a good thing and a positive indicator of effective financial management. However, it is important not to be lulled into a state of complacency just because Net Worth is increasing. There may still be room for improvement to boost Net Worth growth even more.

Net Worth Will REMAIN STEADY and FLUCTUATE ONLY SLIGHTLY

If the flow of money in is about equal to the flow of money out, and financial holdings remain steady in value, then Net Worth will remain mostly unchanged. This may or may not be an acceptable trend and often indicates room for improving overall financial management and efficiency.

Net Worth Will DECREASE

Finally, if the flow of money out exceeds the flow of money in, and/or there is a drop in the value of financial holdings, then Net Worth will obviously decline. Depending on where a person is in life, this can be either a bad trend or simply a normal trend that bears watching.

It is a bad trend for younger people in their working years and indicates either poor financial management or an event or unusual circumstance that is draining their financial resources or causing a decline in the value of financial holdings. In any case, it is a trend that if left unchecked, will lead to financial problems or even disaster, sometimes in the form of bankruptcy or other type of insolvency.

For people in retirement, declining Net Worth is not necessarily a problem, because when a person retires it is not unusual for them to have a reduction in money flowing in. First, they may be receiving less income during retirement than in their working years, which often necessitates making withdrawals from investments to supplement income, decreasing the value of these assets.

Second, they may have reallocated their investment funds to a more conservative investment mix, which typically decreases investment returns, while at the same time limiting investment losses during times of stock market volatility. The combination of decreased income and lower investment returns, together with maintaining their standard of living over the many years of retirement, can and often does cause a decline in Net Worth during retirement.

It is essential to keep track of Net Worth during retirement and carefully and systematically manage it, so that it does not decline to the point that you run out of money, forcing you to make sacrifices or reductions in your standard of living and desired retirement lifestyle.

This is why I have my clients establish a benchmark Net Worth number. This number is used as a reference going forward to track how Net Worth is trending over time: up, unchanged, or declining.

For example, let's say a person's/couple's benchmark Net Worth is calculated to be $750,000. One year later, their Net Worth has increased to $800,000. It can be assumed, on initial inspection, that over the previous twelve months their money was managed effectively. If, on the other hand, their Net Worth has remained unchanged or has declined, corresponding conclusions can be drawn from these results.

Each time I meet with my clients, we update their balance sheet and inspect their Net Worth, then compare it to the benchmark Net Worth number. Based on this exercise, we then proceed accordingly.

Therefore, depending on where you are in life, you will want to set an expectation for how you want your Net Worth to trend. If you are still in your working years, you want your Net Worth to be trending up or, at the very least, staying about the same. If you are retired, you may be perfectly satisfied with Net Worth that is remaining mostly unchanged, or even declining. Remember, if your Net Worth declines, it is not necessarily cause for alarm or panic, but you must be vigilant to make sure it is not declining at an unsafe rate.

I describe it to my clients this way: *"Think of your Net Worth like a plane. During your working years you take off and ascend to your desired cruising altitude (lifestyle). When you retire, you begin your descent. During your descent, you must have a clear view of the gauges that track and report your altitude (net worth), so you can control your rate of descent. If you see at any time that you are descending too quickly, you can take steps to correct your course and slow your descent so you don't end up crashing (running out of money). A controlled descent will help you make a pinpoint landing. If the plane descends to quickly, you will come in short of the runway and crash. You don't want to crash, right? Of course not, so it is essential that you track your descent for a pinpoint landing. This is not only important for you, but it is also important to all those on board your plane, like your family, who depend on you to land safely."* A little hokey perhaps, but it always gets the point across.

In any case, the financial organization step is about completing a careful inventory of all your assets and liabilities and establishing your benchmark Net Worth that will serve as your starting point for monitoring your financial progress.

Step 3

Analyze Investments

The individual investor should act consistently as an investor and not as a speculator. –Ben Graham

This step is about conducting a thorough review of all your assets, both liquid and non-liquid, so you have a complete understanding of how your assets are performing and if they are doing what you expected or hoped for. The objective is to determine if assets should remain where they are or be re-allocated, re-balanced, and/or re-purposed.

The areas of review in this step include:

- Return on investment performance
- Portfolio allocation of stock market holdings and risk analysis
- Fees for portfolio management and advice
- Tax allocation of assets
- Liquidity

Let's look at these one at a time.

Return on investment performance

This represents the rate of return received on an invested asset over time. It is simply a calculation of the appreciation or depreciation of the value of an asset over a particular timeframe. This is obviously important to know in terms of assessing the overall effectiveness of an investment strategy. However, I do want to caution people about being too focused on the numbers.

Rate of return on any investment or other invested funds or assets is often the only measure taken by people regarding their money. They follow the performance of their investments according to a value and/or percentage increase or decrease. Typically, they obtain a report showing that a particular account or holding increased or decreased by some value or percentage amount and they use this to assess the effectiveness of their money management. People want to invest their dollars and find more dollars in the future. This makes sense.

If the value of one's investments go up or down, this would seem to be *the* most effective way to measure the success of a money management plan or strategy. However, even though this is reasonable and sensible in principle, it often leads people to be excessively and narrowly focused on the ups and downs of the stock market, and prone to attempting something generally referred to as "market timing" which is the practice of trying to figure out when the market will move up or down and then make investment decisions to buy and sell at the most opportune time.

I do not want to delve into a long discussion of the effectiveness of this particular investment strategy, but there have been studies evaluating how effective market timing has been for the average investor, and the numbers are not that good. Suffice it to say that for the average investor, trying to figure out the tops and bottoms of stock market cycles has actually been a costly activity. It is important to remember that being out of the market and having money sitting on the sidelines waiting for the "right time" to reinvest means possibly missing good days when the market is up.

Of course, this also means missing bad days, but consider this. Using the S&P 500 Index, if a person invested $10,000 on January 1, 1997 and left it fully invested until December 30, 2016, it grew to $43,933, a 7.68% return. On the other hand, if the investor missed the best ten days in the market, their rate of return dropped almost in half to $21,925, a 4.00%

return). Noteworthy here is that six of the ten best days occurred within two weeks of the worst ten market days. Also noteworthy—this time period included the Dot Com Crash and the 2008 Financial Crisis.

While it is important to monitor performance of your investments, it is also important to assess performance based on your objectives, or what you want your money to accomplish for you, rather than simply on performance or rate of return numbers.

This is often difficult for many to understand and accept, because the financial services industry is always throwing performance numbers at us with little else. It's certainly important to grow your money, but it's equally as important to set and achieve investment objectives that act as a guide for measuring investment success. Investment objectives relate back to Step 1: *Envision Your Retirement.*

What I hope you will better understand and appreciate going forward is that investment performance is important, but it is not the sole measure of how effectively your money is being managed.

● Portfolio allocation of stock market holdings and risk analysis

Investing in the stock market is a risky proposition, but how a portfolio is allocated will determine the level of risk. The essential stock market risk categories are, from highest to lowest:

I will not devote time to describe these categories and the target allocations that typically comprise each, but I do want to make the point that as people approach and live in retirement, they should be reallocating and rebalancing their investment portfolios to be more conservative. This will serve to minimize losses in the event of a stock market correction or crash as you approach and enter retirement.

Conservative portfolios typically are comprised of a higher percentage of bonds than stocks or equities, but there are numerous allocation models that can help to protect a portfolio from stock market volatility that do not depend on the ratio of stocks to bonds. Personally, I am also a believer in high quality, blue chip dividend paying stocks as a way to hedge against market volatility; but again, I am not going to go into detail on this in this publication.

The importance of doing a thorough review of your current portfolio allocations is to determine your level of exposure to potential future stock market corrections or crashes. For retirees, taking a large loss, or any loss for that matter, just before or during retirement can and often will curtail retirement plans and alter lifestyle goals.

● Fees for portfolio management and advice

The reality is that the financial services, investment, and insurance companies are for-profit enterprises. Likewise, the people who work for these companies in sales, advisory, support, and administrative capacities are trying to earn a paycheck and make a living. Subsequently, fees and other charges are necessary to generate the needed revenue for these companies to earn a profit and compensate their employees. Selling investment management services, and investment and insurance products is how these fees are generated.

This seems obvious and simple enough, but most of us still grimace at the prospect of paying fees for financial products and services. After all, no one likes paying fees. On the other hand, it's like the old adage: "You get what you pay for." In other words, if you receive a product or service that is of high quality and value, then you should not mind paying a commensurate fee or cost for it. I recently went to New York City and had lunch at the 2nd Avenue Deli. The service was great and the deli sandwich I was served was absolutely delectable. It was also more than $20 and is, to the best of my recollection, the most expensive sandwich I have ever purchased. However, I happily paid the check and left the waiter a generous tip because it was well worth it! Consequently, the next time I go to NYC, I will be returning to the 2nd Avenue Deli for lunch and will be happy to pay the check, despite the higher cost. I do not mind paying a higher fee for a product or service, as long as I feel the price is justified.

This is just one example of a time when the cost of a product or service was worth it. On the other hand, I have purchased products and services that were absolutely not worth it, and in some instances were an absolute rip-off. In the financial services industries, there are certainly examples of high quality products and services that absolutely justify the fees and costs, and likewise, there are all kinds of rip-offs.

In the case of my deli sandwich, it was quite easy to arrive at a conclusion regarding whether the sandwich was worth the higher price—the bread was fresh and soft, and the meat was inches thick and very tasty! However, with investment and insurance products and services, it is not quite as clear as to whether the fees are justified, or worth it. In fact, it can be very difficult to even know what fees are being charged.

Because the financial services and insurance industries deliver so many different kinds of products and services in so many different ways and over extended periods of time, fee ambiguity is a huge problem. For example, do you know what fees are being charged for your 401k or 403b retirement savings account? I have actually had people tell me they are not being charged any fees for their employer sponsored retirement savings plan, thinking it is a free employee benefit. The truth is that these financial products are among the most expensive and fee-laden, and it's not just retirement plans. You are paying fees and other charges on every single investment, bank, and insurance product you own. Not that this is a bad thing, because again, all the companies and people that provide these products and related services must be financially remunerated. I contend that it is not the fee or charge we incur that we object to, but whether the fee is worth it.

I refer to this part of the planning process as "fee discovery" because few if anyone has a good or clear idea of what they are paying in fees and charges on the investment and insurance products they own. If they do, it is vague at best. It is also an involved task to discover what is being charged, because in many cases, the companies and people providing the products and services are unclear what is being charged. Just ask anyone in your HR department about 401k fees, and nine times out of ten, they can't answer the question because they simply do not know.

This is why fee discovery is an important part of the planning process. Not necessarily because you want to escape paying fees, but because you want to be able to assess if the fees you are paying are worth it. It's also important to note that fees, even at what may seem a small or an insignificant amount, can add up over time and end up being a big number. So although you will be charged fees for products and services you receive, you want to ask these three questions:

What fees are you paying?
How much are these fees, and are they based on a flat rate or percentage?
Are you receiving a fair value in return for the fees you are paying? Are they "worth it"?

Here is a general description of typical fees and charges you may come across for investment and/or insurance products.

Expense Ratio

This fee is common to mutual funds and offsets the costs to formulate and manage a fund. It is a recurring operating expense that is calculated based on the percentage of the value of the amount invested. A fund with an expense ratio of 1.0% means that for every $1,000 invested, $10 per year will go to the fund management company for their services in operating the fund and managing the fund's holdings.

Typically, the expense ratio is deducted from your account balance by the fund management company or custodian, so you never see a bill for this.

The expense ratio will vary depending on the company and fund type. Generally, funds that require less management (passive management) have lower expense ratios, such as an Index Fund or Exchange Traded Fund. These types of funds incur fewer if any trades and fluctuate more on the ups and downs of the overall market or index. Conversely, funds that are more actively or tactically managed will have higher expense ratios. This is due to the fund manager spending more time and resources to research which holdings a fund should acquire to maximize rates of return and achieve investment objectives.

In an *Investopedia* article update on December 20, 2018, J.B. Maverick explains, "The average expense ratio for actively managed mutual funds is between 0.5% and 1.0% and typically goes no higher than 2.5%, although some fund ratios have gone higher. For passive index funds, the typical ratio is approximately 0.2%."

Obviously, the lower the expense ratio, the lower the cost. However, it can be tricky to simply decide to invest in a particular fund based on the expense ratio, although many will argue this is the primary factor, and with some people it is the only factor to consider. I do not want to digress into a discussion of passive versus active portfolio management, but the investment philosophy you advocate will play into how much you ultimately pay in expense ratio fees on your investments.

Investment Management or Advisory Fees

These fees compensate a company and/or individual for advice and services related to the management of an investment portfolio, typically stocks, bonds, and/or mutual funds. The amount paid is generally charged as a percentage of the total assets under management. For example, if a financial or investment advisor charges 1.0% of the total value of a portfolio or the amount being managed, this would equate to $1,000 annually for $100,000 invested. This fee is most commonly debited from the account on a quarterly basis, so in this example it would be $250 per quarter.

An advisory or management fee can range from 0.25% to 3% on average depending on the level of services offered. It also will vary based on the size of the portfolio, with a lower percentage fee charged on larger portfolios, typically in excess of $1,000,000.

In many cases this fee only covers advice related to portfolio management, but there are firms that include additional services including financial planning, tax planning, estate planning, budgeting assistance, etc.

Transaction Fee

This type of fee is charged to cover trading fees that are incurred each time an order to buy or sell a mutual fund or stock is placed. These fees can range from less than $10 per trade to over $50 per trade. If you are investing small amounts of money, these fees add up quickly.

Front-End Load

A front-end load is a commission or sales charge applied at the time an initial investment is made, typically with mutual funds and some types of life insurance policies. It is deducted from the amount invested and, as a result, reduces the amount of money that goes directly into the investment. This fee is charged to pay up-front costs such as sales commissions. The type of shares that incur a front-end load are referred to as "A" shares. For example, if you invest in a mutual fund with a front-end load of 5%, 5¢ of each dollar invested is immediately deducted, with the remaining 95¢ going into the investment. In this case, your investment must earn 5.26% over the next year to get back to the original amount invested.

In addition to "A" shares, there are "B" shares, which also charge a load, but it is collected on the back end if the shares are redeemed within a specified period of time. If B shares are held long enough, then the load expires and is not charged upon redemption. There is another class of shares worth mentioning called "C" shares, which have neither a front- or back-end load, but have a higher expense ratio than A and B shares.

Annual Account Fee or Custodian Fee

Brokerage accounts and mutual fund accounts typically charge an annual account fee, which can range from $25 to $90 per year on average. An annual custodian fee is typically charged on retirement accounts, such as IRA's, which covers the IRS reporting that is required on these types of accounts. This fee typically ranges from $10 to $50 per year. You may also incur an account-closing fee that can range from $25 to $150 per account upon redeeming all funds in an account.

Surrender Charges

This charge is common to life insurance and annuity products and is deducted from cash value if a policy is surrendered or cashed in early. The surrender charge period will vary depending on the company and the particular product, and can range from just a few years to as many as twenty or more years. In most cases, the surrender charge will be a percentage of the policy's cash value and will decrease each year until it goes to $0. Be sure to check the length and terms of your surrender charge when evaluating a policy to buy.

● Tax allocation of assets

Taxes are perhaps the largest ongoing expense you will incur in retirement, and will likely have more impact on your retirement savings and cash flow than any other single expense. Yet, this is an area of planning that is often not prioritized by many retirees. This is not to suggest retirees are not concerned about taxes, quite the contrary. But it does suggest a disconnect between what people need to do for retirement planning and what they typically seek out or receive from retirement planners. It may also suggest people are confused about how to go about managing their taxes, or have simply resigned themselves to paying the taxes their annual tax return indicates must be paid. In any case, with the right kind of planning, reducing taxes during retirement is a real possibility.

Retirement tax planning is extremely complex and requires a very specific process, but it starts with an understanding of how each retirement income and asset resource will be taxed. There are three possibilities:

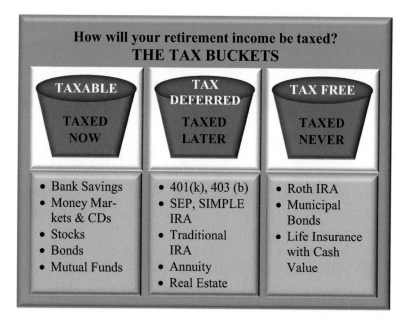

How will your retirement income be taxed? **THE TAX BUCKETS**		
TAXABLE	**TAX DEFERRED**	**TAX FREE**
TAXED NOW	**TAXED LATER**	**TAXED NEVER**
• Bank Savings • Money Markets & CDs • Stocks • Bonds • Mutual Funds	• 401(k), 403 (b) • SEP, SIMPLE IRA • Traditional IRA • Annuity • Real Estate	• Roth IRA • Municipal Bonds • Life Insurance with Cash Value

A *taxable* asset is one where the gains are taxed on an annual basis. These include traditional bank accounts, including Certificate of Deposit, savings, and money market accounts that earn interest. Earnings from bonds and dividends fall here as well, with some exceptions.

A *tax deferred* asset is comprised of money from employment wages that have not yet been taxed and will accumulate tax deferred until distribution, at which time the funds will be taxed as ordinary income. The types of accounts included here are Individual Retirement Account (IRA), 401(k), 403(b), and Simplified Employee Pension (SEP), just to mention the more common types. It is also noteworthy that other assets, such as a real estate and non-tax qualified annuities have aspects of tax deferral.

A *tax-exempt or tax-free* asset is a particular type of account that was funded with money from employment wages that have already been taxed. These include: Roth IRA, Roth 401(k), and withdrawals from cash value life insurance (tax exempt up to basis in policy).

As a result of the popularity of Traditional IRAs, 401k, 403b, and other tax deferred savings plans over the past several decades, the majority of retirement funds are held in tax deferred accounts. Since the early 1980s, people have been accumulating these funds and enjoying the benefits of putting off paying taxes until after age 59½, presumably when retired and taking distributions.

The benefit of this is fairly straight forward—money that would otherwise go to income taxes goes instead into investments that hopefully grow over time. Very simply, people end up with larger retirement account balances due to deferring the payment of taxes on a portion of their wages. It would seem, based on the trillions of dollars accumulated in tax deferred retirement accounts that this has worked well.

However, something else has accumulated over the years which is not so good—a deferred tax bill that is perhaps larger than many realize or expect. This means the number representing your account balance staring back at you from your retirement account statement is not all yours; a piece of it belongs to Uncle Sam.

In a sense, there is a tax lien on the funds in your retirement account, and it must be paid. The problem you need to solve is *when* you will pay the taxes and *how much* you or your heirs will end up paying. There are various tax rules that must be followed to avoid penalties, but there are also options to consider to reduce the amount of taxes you ultimately pay.

You should start by determining how much of your retirement nest egg resides in each of the three tax categories. There are also strategies including Roth Conversions and optimizing income and reducing taxes by properly sequencing income sources and account distributions. Also carefully review Social Security claiming options and how retirement income can impact the taxation of your Social Security.

This is an area of complexity that requires a deeper dive and one-on-one work with a qualified professional, but remember the old adage: *"It's not how much you have that really counts, but how much you keep."*

Liquidity

Liquidity has to do with your ability to access and utilize your funds within selected accounts without incurring a penalty or surrender charge. It is fairly common for financial and insurance companies to restrict access to funds for a period of time for the purpose of enhancing your account benefits and maximizing their profits.

A common example is a Certificate of Deposit (CD) available at most banking institutions. In return for a higher interest rate on a CD account, the depositor must agree to allow the bank to keep their money for a minimum specified period of time. If the depositor withdraws funds early, the banking institution charges a penalty.

Other examples include certain types of annuities, cash value life insurance, and mutual funds with a Contingent Deferred Sales Charge (B Shares).

It is also important to understand that your access to funds invested in tax qualified investments such as an IRA (traditional, Roth & SIMPLE), 401(k), 403(b), SEP, etc. will be severely limited until you reach age 59½. There will be a 10% penalty imposed on your federal taxes if you withdraw funds before this age. (Note that IRA owners under age 59½ can avoid the 10% early withdrawal penalty if they elect to withdraw the funds by using a series of substantially equal periodic payments. The payments must continue for a period of five years or until 59½, whichever comes later. Refer to IRS Code §72(t) for specific details.) In addition, ordinary income taxes will be due in the year of an early withdrawal from an IRA or other tax deferred account.

Liquidity or full access to your money is certainly preferred, but not always necessary, especially with your longer term investments. It may be perfectly acceptable to invest in certain types of savings vehicles that restrict access to your money, based on the additional benefits being offered. However, be certain that you have a clear understanding of how long the restriction will last and make sure that the funds will not be needed before this. It is also essential that you maintain a specific amount of liquid funds for both short term needs and unexpected needs and events, otherwise referred to as "emergency money."

Step 4

Manage Cash Flow

Staying positive…

This step is about developing a plan to manage the dollars flowing in and the dollars flowing out and how this flow of dollars ultimately impacts your retirement savings.

Dollars flowing in can be from numerous sources: wages, distributions from retirement and other investment accounts, Social Security, pensions, interest, dividends, real estate, etc. Dollars flowing out are for covering living expenses and activities related to the requirements and choices around your lifestyle. Essentially, this is about cash flow and how your cash flow ultimately impacts your overall savings and investments, or more aptly, your net worth.

Earlier I described being proactive versus reactive regarding your planning. It is the same with your cash flow management. The vast majority of us are reactive with our spending to the extent that as money flows in, we tend to quickly turn it around so it flows out to pay bills and other spending based on what is at the top of our mind and seemingly important. In other words, who or whatever is tugging at our coattails for money gets paid first. This can work as long as there is a consistently positive cash flow.

However, this method of cash flow management (using this term loosely) is almost never efficient, and typically leads to wasting money. Achieving an effective cash flow routine that will have you saving and spending efficiently is a tall order for many due to long standing spending habits, but it is achievable and simpler than you may think. It requires prioritizing your expenses according to importance and categories.

There are two essential spending categories: *living expenses and discretionary expenses*

Items you...

MUST SPEND MONEY ON
- Housing
- Groceries, Household, Personal Care
- Transportation
- Healthcare

WANT TO SPEND MONEY ON
- Entertainment, Travel
- Family
- Second Home, a Boat, etc.
- Your Bucket List

Living expenses are essential and, for the most part, unavoidable. You will incur these expenses at every stage of life, including retirement, and you must have a cash flow or spending plan to account for these expenses regardless of circumstances.

Discretionary expenses are exactly that—discretionary. They are subject to your discretion and voluntary. Discretionary spending will be quite different for everyone and will be based on personal interests, ambitions, beliefs, etc. In popular culture this is often referred to as your "bucket list."

The ups and downs...

During retirement, is it important to understand that *living* and *discretionary expenses* will trend in different directions over the course of many years.

Living expenses will trend up. Part of this will be the result of increases in the costs of many if not most items needed to maintain your standard of living; this is referred to as "inflation." But the largest and most unpredictable increase in living expenses will likely be related to healthcare. Costs for healthcare will rise due to annual increases in insurance premiums and the overall cost of receiving healthcare, both preventative and needs based.

Healthcare inflation has been escalating and is projected to continue at rates much higher than regular inflation. According to the federal government's Bureau of Labor & Statistics, healthcare inflation has been trending in the 4%+ range, but according to other private research organizations I have reviewed, healthcare costs are escalating at 6% to 8% annually. Regardless of which sources you choose to believe, retirees will see costs double or triple over a thirty-plus years retirement time frame. This trend is further exacerbated by the fact that as people age, they tend to require more healthcare. In fact, the most expensive years of retirement are the last few years because this is typically when the most healthcare will be needed.

Conversely, discretionary expenses will trend down. I am going to borrow a phrase I picked up from Tom Hegna, a retirement planning professional and author on the subject. He talks about the years of retirement segmented into the "go-go" years, "slow-go" years, and "no-go" years.

During the initial "go-go" years of retirement, people are typically on the go. They are traveling, working, volunteering, enjoying hobbies, etc. During the middle "slow-go" retirement years, people tend to scale back on some of their activities as they mark things off their bucket list and slow down due to age and sometimes health. During the final "no-go" years of retirement, age and health related issues tend to moderate or halt retirement activities and related expenses. This trend from "go-go" to "no-go" means less will be spent on discretionary expenses over time.

For the purposes of planning your cash flow over the course of your retirement, which will likely be two to three decades or more, it is important to understand how your living and discretionary expenses are likely to trend.

A lifetime guarantee…

When it comes to properly funding both living and discretionary expenses, it is important to recognize the distinction between guaranteed and non-guaranteed streams of income.

Guaranteed income originates from sources that you can reasonably expect will continue without interruption regardless of personal and/or economic circumstances. Examples of guaranteed streams of income are Social Security, pension, annuity payments, and interest income from funds not at risk.

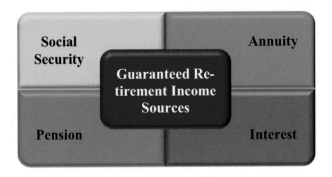

When it comes to retirement income planning, I believe it is prudent to be somewhat selective when identifying income sources for this category, due to longer retirement time frames. In other words, you do not want to count income that has a chance of running out before you "run out." (As a quick caveat to the items above, this assumes that the entities funding these guaranteed income sources, such as federal and state governments, companies, banks, and insurance companies will remain solvent over time. If this is not the case, we all have much bigger problems!)

With regard to the four items I identify as guaranteed income, I want to explain why I believe these are dependable.

Social Security

As we all know, Social Security is a government entitlement program that the vast majority of retired workers will receive. It may seem that the options here are straight forward and simple, but understanding all the options and deciding on a claiming strategy is actually fairly complex in terms of when to begin collecting and how best to coordinate it with a spouse's Social Security benefits. There may also be questions for those who are divorced or whose spouse is deceased.

As part of my planning practice, I do quite a lot of work helping my clients sort out their Social Security claiming options, but for our purposes, I want to address the concern that Social Security will run out of money in the not-too-distant future, leaving its recipients without their benefits.

While it is certainly true that Social Security, along with other government entitlement programs such as Medicare and Medicaid, are at the mercy of Uncle Sam's mounting financial difficulties, the fact is that even if the Social Security Trust Fund does run out of money, all those entitled to Social Security benefits will continue to receive their checks. Benefits are paid through payroll taxes collected from current workers and their employers, and the program currently operates with a surplus of about $2.8 trillion.

However, as more and more retirees join the roles of Social Security (a trend being exacerbated by the Baby Boomers), together with fewer workers paying into the system, the combined Social Security trust funds that supply retirement and disability benefits are projected to exhaust their cash reserves by 2034. That doesn't mean Social Security would be bankrupt and unable to pay benefits.

According to recent Social Security Trustee Reports, Social Security will be able to pay out 79% of benefits until 2090. This assumes Congress does nothing between now and then to prop up the system. I believe Congress will step in and make necessary changes, just as it did back in the early 1980s when Congress acted on behalf of Social Security. The Social Security Amendments of 1983 increased the full retirement age from 65 to 67 for younger workers and imposed taxes on Social Security benefits based on income levels. Obviously, there is no way to predict what Congress will do with Social Security in the future, but the program is too important to simply allow it to run out of money.

Pension

Pensions (also referred to as "Defined Benefit Plans") will comprise a smaller percentage of retirement income for current and future generations than for previous generations. There was a time before the 1980s that a pension was almost a given as an employee benefit for those working in both private and government sectors. However, with the advent of the Defined Contribution Plan, such as the 401k, 403b, SIMPLE IRA, SEP IRA, etc., there has been a pronounced shift away from pensions.

The percentage of workers in the private sector whose only retirement account is a defined benefit pension plan is now 4%, down from 60% in the early 1980s. About 14% of companies offer both defined benefit and defined contribution plans, but these are dwindling as well. In the not-too-distant future, pensions will have gone the way of drive-in movies and 8-track tapes. For those who still have pensions and can include these as part of their retirement income, the issue is dependability.

It is important for every pension recipient to determine if the company or government entity paying their pension will have the resources to honor their pension obligations in full. Unfortunately, there are companies that have not properly funded their pension liabilities. In some cases, people who were promised pensions and planned their retirements accordingly were cheated out of the money they were expecting. The reasons for this range from companies miscalculating their ability to fund pension liabilities with ongoing revenues, to outright corporate fraud.

There is also concern that some municipalities will have difficulty funding their future pension obligations. According to various estimates, the largest municipal pension plans have unfunded pension liabilities exceeding $500 billion. In addition, states carry unfunded pension obligations of as much as $3 trillion.

Companies, municipalities, and states with unfunded pension promises will have to pay retired workers from ongoing revenues, and in an era when there is growing demand on revenues and pressure to cut taxes and fees, this may be difficult for some, leading to some retirees not receiving what they expected and were promised.

If you are expecting a pension, do some work to confirm the financial soundness of the entity that will be making your payments. You can also contact the Pension Benefit Guaranty Corporation (www.pbgc.gov), which is an independent federal agency overseen by the Department of Labor.

Annuity

Annuities come in many varieties and can be very confusing. In my travels though the financial services and insurance industries, I find that annuities are among the most confusing and misunderstood of all financial/insurance products, but I will not use this publication to list and explain all the various types of annuities and their uses. What you should understand is that an annuity can provide an income stream payable monthly or annually for a specified length of time or the rest of one's life.

These payments are made by a life insurance company and are guaranteed. You might ask why I consider payments from a life insurance company to be *guaranteed*, and my answer is that these companies are among the most financially solvent of all corporate entities, not to mention that most have the financial backing of state sponsored insurance guarantee funds.

How life insurance works to guarantee payments for a person's remaining life, regardless of how long that person may live, has a lot to do with actuarial tables and mortality credits, which I will not delve into here. Suffice it to say that an annuity contract from a reputable life insurance company is as guaranteed as anything reasonably can be.

Interest

Income from interest comes primarily from banks and bonds. The extent to which this income can be considered guaranteed depends on the entity paying it and the funds on which the interest payments are being earned. In the case of banks, the government, by way of the FDIC, guarantees the safety of principle up to certain thresholds. So if one is able to maintain a set amount within a particular bank account, the interest earned will continue.

Likewise, with bonds, the interest earned will be consistent assuming the funds remain constant. However, there are many varieties of bonds payable by different private and government entities, so it is incumbent upon the recipient to carefully examine the process and options for investing in bonds.

It should be understood that regardless of how you earn interest income, fluctuating interest rates will influence the amount of income received over time.

They say there are no guarantees in life…

Non-guaranteed income are sources that could run out, be diminished, or be negatively impacted by personal and/or economic circumstances. Examples here include wages from jobs held during retirement, withdrawals from retirement savings, and other income from stock market holdings. Eventually, everyone will reach a point they can no longer hold down a job, and retirement savings and stock market holdings are subject to investment risk that can diminish their value and income over time.

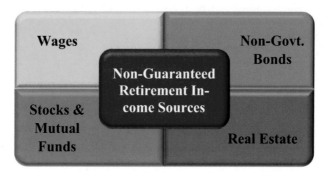

A retirement income plan should be designed so that living expenses are paid using guaranteed income sources, and discretionary expenses should mostly come from non-guaranteed sources or funds set aside specifically for discretionary spending.

How does one go about developing a retirement spending or a cash flow plan along the lines of living and discretionary expenses, using guaranteed and non-guaranteed income streams? It certainly is a challenge, but if you begin by organizing and understanding your asset and income resources, then you will be well on your way. This will help you properly prioritize and sequence your income and spending such that you will maximize cash flow efficiency. Ultimately you want the most income possible with the least exposure to taxes and other income eroding factors.

All of this starts with prioritizing spending according to what is most important, and doing it according to a specific hierarchy that is in line with your objectives. This will obviously be different for everyone depending on circumstances, goals, and stages of life, but there are essential principles that apply to everyone.

Very simply, living expenses are prioritized over discretionary expenses, with guaranteed income streams being used primarily for living expenses and non-guaranteed income streams going for discretionary expenses. Certainly, there will be some overlap and exceptions, but the principle is sound and should serve you well as a guideline to managing your cash flow.

Step 5

Mitigate Retirement Risks

Hope for the best, but plan for the worst…

The first four steps of the process have led us to the point that we have developed a basic retirement plan. This plan, however, is based on two essential elements:

> ***What you know right now***
> ***What you hope and expect will happen in the future***

In other words, your planning is based on what you know about your life and the economy as they stand today. Since none of us has a crystal ball, we can't make plans based on what *will* happen in the future, only on what we *hope and expect will* happen in the future. What if the things you hope and expect will happen, don't happen?

Let's use an example from the fairly recent past—the 2008 Financial Crisis. Many people lost a lot of personal wealth as the stock and real estate markets collapsed back in 2008. Many people on the verge of retirement had to delay retiring due to the financial losses they experienced.

Prior to the collapse, the markets were doing great and providing big returns to investors. No one saw the collapse coming, and when it hit, many would-be retirees ended up taking big losses at exactly the time they couldn't afford to. I contend that if they had planned properly, those pre- and post-retirees that took big losses in 2008 would have preserved much of what they lost. It wasn't about not knowing the financial crisis was coming; it was about not being properly allocated in the event a collapse did occur.

This is just one example of a risk people face in retirement, namely "stock market risk." There are certainly other risks in addition to this one to contend with. Although retirement planning is the process of deciding what you want and then managing the resources needed to achieve and support the plan, it is also about understanding and anticipating what can go wrong with the plan.

You are likely familiar with the phrase adapted from the poem of Robert Burns: "The best laid plans of mice and men often go awry." What this means to me is that you can do all the planning you want in order to attain the things you hope for and expect, but things often go wrong that can subvert even the best conceived plans.

It is not my intention to be a pessimist, but when it comes to planning for retirement, it is prudent to look for risks and then take steps to manage and mitigate the problems that can result from these risks. Growing up, many of us were taught to never go looking for trouble, but with regard to retirement planning, you should not only look for trouble, but stare it right in the face. Do your planning by the old adage, "Hope for the best, but plan for the worst."

With regard to Step 5 in *6 Steps Retirement*, you should understand and accept that risk can never be eliminated, but you can certainly take steps to minimize the impact of retirement risks. Think of it this way—if you do experience a problem, you want it to be a problem you can manage and solve so it doesn't end up being a budget busting, life altering problem. Again, you cannot eliminate risk, but with the right kind of planning you can reduce its impact.

The typical retirement risks I'm referring to include, but are not limited to, the following:

I could write volumes on each of these areas of risk and still not cover all the contingencies, so I won't try, except to offer a short narrative on each.

Stock Market Volatility

When it comes to hope and expectation, the stock market is our panacea. It's where our investment dreams come true; or it's where we experience nightmares. Working with people in the area of investment management, I am well versed on the ups and downs of the stock market, and like to think, as most investment professionals do, that I have a good idea what drives market volatility.

Of course, for every ten Wall Street experts, there are eleven opinions on why the market goes up and down. We would like to think it's rooted in empirical, definable, and trackable terms, but the reality is that much of what drives the market is rooted in human emotion, with fear, hope, and greed leading the charge. In any case, the task at hand is to be in the stock market without risking more than you can afford to lose—which is unfortunately what happened to many in 2008.

When you are younger and have two to four decades ahead of you before retiring, addressing stock market risk is mostly about investing in a well-diversified portfolio of high quality securities, and then staying invested and riding the ups and downs of the market. (Without going into detail, the biggest mistake many long-term stock market investors make is trying to time the market by moving money in and out based on when they think the market is at its lows and highs. Numerous studies correlating returns for those attempting to time the market as opposed to staying invested clearly show market timing does not work.) But for those nearing or in retirement, addressing stock market risk is more about not losing money, or preserving what has been accumulated over many years.

There is no absolute right way to accomplish this. Many investment professionals advocate reallocating money from securities to bonds. Others suggest portfolios of high-quality, Blue-Chip dividend paying securities. Then there are those who preach divesting of all stock market holdings and investing in "safe money" assets such as annuities and life insurance.

Who is right or which strategy is most effective is something that only time will tell. However, there is a wrong way to preserve your money and it has to do with failing to recognize the need to change investment focus at the point of retiring. Too many people invest in their 50s and 60s like they invested in the 20s and 30s. These people focus their investment objective on growing their money, and while this seems very logical given what they have done all their lives and are being told by many investment professionals to keep doing, their investment objective should change to more of an emphasis on income.

There are two essential reasons to invest:

> *Invest for growth*
> *Invest for income*

Investing for growth can take many forms, but will almost always entail some level of investment risk. The greater the return you seek, the greater the risk you must be willing to take, such as being invested in an aggressively allocated stock portfolio.

Investing for income allows for investments in more conservative and safer investments such as bonds, annuities, dividend generating securities, and bank instruments. Of course, your overall investment objectives must be considered according to your own needs and circumstances, but investing for income is a good way to mitigate stock market portfolio risk as you approach and live in retirement.

Inflation

Inflation is perhaps the most serious, yet least discussed, of all the retirement risks. The fact is that every day, week, month, and year for the rest of your life, your money will be losing purchasing power. If you consider this fact over the term of twenty to thirty or more years of retirement, the amount of diminished purchasing power can make maintaining one's standard of living more challenging over time.

As published on November 14, 2018, by USinflationcalculator.com in an article titled "US Inflation Rises 2.5%, Consumer Prices in October Log Biggest Jump in 9 Months," inflation as measured by the Consumer Price Index (CPI) was 2.1% for the 12 months ending October 2018. This number was calculated by the government using what is referred to as a "basket of goods." The basket of goods includes food and beverages, housing costs and other household items such as furniture, apparel, transportation expenses, medical care, and various recreational expenses. Also included are education and communication expenses and some random items such as tobacco, haircuts, and funerals.

Looking at inflation in terms of purchasing power, if inflation continued at 2.1% over a ten-year period, what $1.00 buys today in products and services will buy only 81¢ worth in ten years. In twenty years, that dollar will buy only 65¢ worth, and in thirty years, only 53¢—assuming inflation continues to average a rate that in the not-too-distant past has certainly been higher. (Many of us can recall much higher inflation rates, such as 12.3% in 1974, 13.3% in 1979, and 12.4% in 1980.)

I don't mean to suggest that we will return to higher inflation rates anytime soon, but based on how freely the Federal Reserve has been increasing the money supply (printing money) in recent years to help the economy along, higher rates of inflation are certainly possible. (These programs are also known as Economic Stimulus Packages and Quantitative Easings 1, 2, and 3.)

My main point with regard to inflation as a retirement risk is that there is very little mention of this in the media or by the political elite, translating into little if any concern among the current and soon to be retired. In other words, we are taking for granted that inflation will stay low and that diminished purchasing power, even at continued low inflation rates, is not, for most, a retirement planning priority. We certainly hope inflation will remain low, but to expect this will be the case and plan accordingly could end up being a big mistake for many.

Rising Healthcare Costs

Healthcare costs will trend two ways during your retirement. The first is the natural increase in the costs of healthcare products and services due to inflation. The second is a person's need for additional healthcare products and services due to aging.

Unfortunately as we age, our health diminishes, and the need for doctors, hospitals, medications, etc increases, especially as the quality of medical products and services improve with time and technology to keep people living longer than in the past.

This means most people will need to account for escalating healthcare expenses as they age. This is further exacerbated by the current state of confusion and indecisiveness at the policy level with regard to health insurance by the government (Medicare and Medicaid), and private sector insurance companies.

We are all aware of ObamaCare (Patient Protection and Affordable Care Act) and what a politically divisive issue it has become. How this will play out over time and the impact it will have on the ongoing cost of healthcare for Americans is anybody's guess.

The bottom line is that the unpredictable nature of what healthcare inflation will be, together with how much healthcare an individual will need over their retirement years makes this an important area of retirement planning.

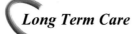

Long Term Care

The odds are against you…

Long term care is easy to classify as a retirement risk due to the high likelihood that a person will need it. In fact, the statistics are downright scary!

According to AARP, the probability of experiencing difficulty performing at least two activities of daily living or becoming cognitively impaired is 68%—more than two-thirds of all people age 65 and older. [Beyond 50. 2003: A Report to the Nation on Independent Living and Disability, 2003, (11 Jan 2005).] From a statistical perspective, that means that you are more likely than not to need some type of long term care. This naturally begs the question, *what exactly is long term care?*

We are all familiar with nursing homes and assisted living facilities. The people who reside in these places are unable to perform one or more of the six "Activities of Daily Living," or ADLs:

> *Transferring: the ability to move from one stationary location to another, such as moving from a bed to a chair. Essentially, this is basic mobility within one's living space.*
>
> *Bathing: the ability to maintain personal hygiene.*
>
> *Dressing: the ability to dress and undress as needed.*
>
> *Eating: the ability to prepare meals and/or eat.*
>
> *Toileting: the ability to get in and out of the bathroom.*
>
> *Continence: the ability to maintain control of bowel and bladder functions.*

These are activities most people take for granted, until age or some other physical malady makes it difficult or impossible to perform them. It's at this point assistance is needed, or what is typically referred to as long term care.

The two primary planning concerns regarding long term care are *who?* and *where?* In other words, when a person becomes unable to perform one or more of the ADLs, *who* will step in and provide the care and/or coordinate the care that is needed? And *where* will the care be provided? Let's consider each of these questions.

The *who* can be family members, friends, or professionals. Most people grimace at the thought of receiving assistance with ADLs from family or friends due to the personal nature of some of these activities. On the one hand, it may be fine having spouses, offspring, siblings, or friends help with moving from a bed to a chair or preparing a meal, but receiving assistance with bathing, using the bathroom, or eating from this same group would not be in any way desirable; at least that's how I feel.

That leaves professionals, of which there are many varieties. Some are simply people who are hired to provide basic non-medical custodial care, others are trained medical professionals. Some will come to a person's home or be part of the staff of a nursing or assisted living facility. There are also adult day care centers with staff providing certain aspects of long term care.

The *where* can be one's home or a facility, depending on the type and level of care needed. It is almost universal that people needing long term care prefer to receive it at their home, or what is sometimes referred to as "aging in place." This is usually better from a cost perspective as well since home care will typically be less expensive than care provided in a long term care facility.

When people reach the point of needing care, it will typically be provided in the person's home for as long as possible. What often occurs is the type of care a person needs escalates as part of the aging process or a particular illness, and they reach the point that care can no longer be provided in the home, and a move to a care facility is prescribed. At this point, long term care costs can become prohibitively expensive, which is the financial/retirement risk associated with long term care.

The cost of long term care can be quite high, especially if it's administered in an assisted living or nursing home facility. I'm not going to discuss costs specifically because the range based on need and location is far reaching, but suffice it to say that it can cost well into the five and six figures and can be a real retirement budget buster for many retirees, especially since the need for long term care typically comes later in retirement when financial resources for many have already been stretched.

From a retirement planning perspective, you should plan a way to fund a potential long term care need. The importance of this planning step cannot be overstated. For married couples, the cost of care for a spouse needing assistance can actually impoverish the healthy spouse, and for unmarried or widowed people, a long term care need can deplete or exhaust their funds as well.

In my experience, long term care planning is a low priority for most people, not that they don't recognize the potential need for it, but that they don't appreciate the level of financial risk it presents. According to a 2007 U.S. Census Bureau survey of 959 Americans between the ages of twenty-one and seventy-five years, the vast majority understand their risk of needing long-term care, but underestimate the cost and overestimate Medicare's role in paying for it.

Among the misconceptions in the survey sample are these:

- *7 in 10 think the average cost of nursing home care is $30,000.* This is less than half the actual national average cost of $73,000.
- *40% believe Medicare covers long term care expenses.* Medicare will partially cover the cost of 100

days of recuperative care in a nursing facility under certain conditions, but after 100 days will pay nothing additional.

There are essentially three ways to cover the cost of long term care:

➢ Pay for it out of your own funds, or self-insure.

➢ Have the government pay for it. This is where Medicaid might step in to cover costs. However, Medicaid is a state administered, public assistance program that is needs based. In other words, one must be unable to pay for care out of their own financial resources before Medicaid will step in. This essentially means that one must have depleted their own funds and be essentially broke in order to get Medicaid to pay the bills.

➢ Have it paid for by an insurance company by way of some type of long term care insurance. Based on what is the average long term need of 2 ½ years and the average annual nursing home cost of $73,000, this equates to $182,500 in today's dollars. Since the average age to enter a nursing home for those reaching age 65 is over age 80, the actual cost for today's retirees will be considerably higher. According to the Genworth 2017 Cost of Care Survey, long term care costs are rising annually at a rate of 4.5%. If this continues, the average annual cost of a nursing home in 25 years will be $220,000.

Tax Rate Hikes

The predominant retirement planning principle regarding income taxes is that they will be lower when you retire. This belief originates from the theory that when a person retires they will end up in a lower marginal tax bracket and therefore, pay less in taxes. This seems to make sense considering that most people retire and surrender their paycheck, so their taxable income drops.

I will not directly challenge this thesis, but several factors may, and for many, will offset a reduction in income taxes in retirement.

Giveth, then taketh away...

First, tax rates may actually rise during the several decades many will be retired. The recently passed legislation referred to as the Tax Cuts and Jobs Act lowered tax rates, but only temporarily. In 2025, many of the provisions of this law, including the lower tax rates, are scheduled to expire and revert back to pre-2018 levels. What we need to recognize regarding tax rates is that the national debt of the United States is escalating at a rate not unlike that of a runaway train. Higher tax rates in the future may become a necessity in order to contend with a burgeoning national debt crisis.

Second, while people are younger they typically have tax deductions such as home mortgage interest and child tax credits that many won't have in retirement. This means their taxable income may not be as low as anticipated.

Third, many retirees will be taking distributions from tax deferred retirement accounts to supplement their income. These will be taxed as ordinary income, resulting in higher taxable income and potentially higher tax rates.

Unexpected Events

I include this as a retirement risk simply because it is prudent to understand that things can and almost certainly will happen that we just don't expect. I won't speculate on what these occurrences may be, except to say that these may be modest in nature and be nothing more than annoyances that are quickly resolved, or they may be more challenging, not easily or quickly resolved, and potentially life changing.

The extent to which one of these occurrences is more manageable and resolved more quickly has a lot to do with how well you understand your personal circumstances and are able to anticipate personal, family, and business issues. Again, without speculating, generally the best way to manage unexpected occurrences is by having quick access to funds. Money obviously doesn't solve all problems, but is can certainly go a long way to helping alleviate the impact of many minor and major unexpected events.

Along this line, it is important to have funds set aside that are quickly and easily accessible. There are rules of thumb regarding how much, but at least six to twelve months of living expenses is advisable.

Obviously, it is important to properly assess you own lifestyle circumstances and determine how much you should set aside, but definitely have something available.

Step 6

Plan Your Estate

It's not just for the rich and famous…

When I bring up the subject of estate planning, I am sometimes greeted with looks of confusion or dismissal because many believe estate planning is only for people with "lots and lots of money" or for "famous people." True enough that the rich and famous typically need estate planning services, but equally as true is that we everyday folks need it as well.

I think of estate planning as the cherry on the sundae, the sundae in this analogy being your retirement plan, something you hopefully have worked hard to develop to address your needs. You can certainly consume and enjoy the sundae, but it really isn't complete without the cherry on top.

I am not trying to simplify or to minimize the importance of an estate plan. If you don't have a well-conceived and implemented estate plan, your overall retirement planning could go for naught.

A well-organized retirement plan can and probably will come apart at the seams if a person becomes incapacitated due to illness or injury, and/or when they pass away. You've probably heard about some famous/rich people who died without an estate plan, causing all kinds of financial and family havoc.

An estate plan allows you to clearly and legally communicate your intentions and wishes with regard to your money, assets, and personal choices at a time or times that you are not able to either due to incapacity or death. Failure to provide clear and legal guidance at these times will leave important decisions and choices up to others. This could be family, friends, professional/business associates, and/or legal entities such as judges and mediators.

The main issue and likely problem is that these people may not get it right; they may not know or have a clear understanding of your intentions and desires. With no estate plan to reference, it is left up to them to speculate as to what you would actually have intended.

Worse is the circumstance where there is disagreement among these people, causing fights that can strain relationships and even rip families and businesses apart. It can also become expensive if disagreements rise to the point of hiring legal professionals to help resolve conflicts. In the end, failure to have an estate plan can leave much legal and emotional damage in its wake.

An estate plan can be relatively simple, or it can be extremely complex, depending on your needs, circumstances, and objectives. Accordingly, each person's estate plan will be unique, but should address two primary objectives:

> *Make certain your money and assets go where you intend after you're gone.*
>
> *Make certain you are cared for as you desire if you ever become incapacitated, and that your final wishes are carried out as you desire.*

Simple enough in concept, but certainly more complex in development and execution.

I will not attempt to go into detail as to how to put together an estate plan, but I will offer some primary points:

Gather Essential Documents to Plan Your Estate

Will
Advanced Healthcare Directives
Power of Attorney
Certain Types of Trusts (depending on circumstances and objectives)

Seek the Advice of a Legal Professional or Service

Do not cut corners here. The legal intricacies of an estate plan require careful planning, development, and implementation. If things are not prepared to the highest degree, taking into account all details, your intentions and preferences could be misinterpreted, misappropriated, not properly implemented, or thwarted altogether.

Store All Important Documents and Data Carefully

You want to be certain that the person or people you intend to have manage your estate plan have quick and easy access to all the documents, data, and anything else needed to make sure your estate wishes are carried out accurately and expeditiously. I suggest the use of electronic data storage options in addition to the proper storage of hardcopy documents and data.

Review Your Entire Estate Plan Regularly

Set a specific time frame to sit down with your legal professional to review all aspects of your estate plan. Your personal and overall financial circumstances will change and evolve over time. As this occurs, you will likely need to update your estate plan accordingly. I also want to make mention of reviewing the beneficiary designations on life insurance and annuity policies and retirement savings accounts such as IRA, 401k, 403b, etc. Reviewing and updating these beneficiary designations should be part of your estate plan review.

Communicate Your Intentions

Communicating your intentions to the person or people you designate to manage your estate plan can be delicate depending on when you want these people to know your intentions regarding your money, assets, and healthcare preferences. You may want to communicate certain things in advance, or not until an event such as incapacity or death. Give very careful consideration to this and seek the advice of trusted people and advisors.

Understand that Certain Aspects of Your Estate Will Be Public After Your Death

Probate is a legal process that validates a will in a court of law, establishing it as a public document of a person's estate in the state of their residence or the location of real property at time of death. This authorizes the executor to begin the process of administering the estate, addressing claims, and distributing the property according to the will. The probate process can take time and there will be a cost. A good estate plan can cut the time and cost of probate and help expedite the distribution of money and assets. It is also important to understand the probated Will becomes a public document for any interested person see. If there are things about your estate you would prefer be kept private, you want to communicate this to your legal professional clearly and make this part of your estate planning process.

CONCLUSION

Retirement planning is not easy, but it does not have to be difficult, either. It is a matter of adopting and following a process that will systematically and effectively help you manage your financial resources in a manner that you understand and ultimately feel comfortable with. I hope this book has helped bring a new, or at least updated, perspective on your retirement planning. It was meant to assist you in organizing your planning tasks and executing them in a logical and efficient sequence.

According to my personal observations over my long financial services career, the level of understanding and confidence the average person has regarding their money is nowhere what it should be. If you feel you have a good handle on your finances and feel confident about your financial future, then you are blessed and also in a very small minority. If, on the other hand, you are among the masses that feel underserved and overplayed by the financial, investment, and insurance industries that are much more about profit than performance, following *6 Steps to Retirement* is for you.

As I close out the book, I want to encourage you to take action, or what I am tagging, "The Steps Within the Steps." Think of these as action steps to assist you to use the information in *6 Steps to Retirement* to develop your own personalized retirement plan. Please visit my website, www.6stepsretirement.com, and click the link "**The Steps Within the Steps**." This will take you to a variety of forms, checklists, and information you can utilize to properly and effectively complete your own *6 Steps* process.

Give this process much thought and reflection, provide a good measure of hard work, make a commitment to consistent reviews and updates, sustain the discipline to stick with it and see it through, and in time I am confident you will establish a predictable, sufficient, and sustainable cash flow that will enable you to achieve and support your desired retirement lifestyle.

Thank you for reading my book and may you retire well and prosper…

1

ENVISION YOUR RETIREMENT

Make a list of all the things you've dreamed about doing and having during your life. Retirement planning isn't just about the money; it's also about what you want to accomplish with your money.

2

ORGANIZE FINANCES

Know what you have…, where it is…, and how much it's all worth…

3

ANALYZE INVESTMENTS

Assess performance against relevant benchmarks; what fees you are paying; how your investments will be taxed; your asset allocation relative to stock market risk.

4

MANAGE CASH FLOW

Leverage your income and asset resources into a retirement cash flow that will provide a predictable, sufficient, and sustainable income to support your desired retirement lifestyle.

5

MITIGATE RETIREMENT RISKS

Identify strategies to mitigate risks that can disrupt or devastate your retirement plans and lifestyle. >Stock market losses >Rising healthcare costs >Inflation >Long term care >Tax rate hikes >Unexpected events

6

PLAN YOUR ESTATE

Establish a plan so more of your money goes to your heirs and not to taxes or nursing homes.
Create Advanced Directives so your healthcare and end of life wishes are carried out as you desire.

36974302R00038

Made in the USA
Middletown, DE
22 February 2019